Beautiful Bathrooms

Tina Skinner

Schiffer Publishing Ltd®

4880 Lower Valley Road, Atglen, PA 19310 USA

Designed by Bonnie M. Hensley
Cover design by Bruce M. Waters
Type set in Zurich LtXCn BT/Zurich BT
ISBN: 0-7643-1536-6
Printed in China

Published by Schiffer Publishing Ltd.
4880 Lower Valley Road
Atglen, PA 19310
Phone: (610) 593-1777; Fax: (610) 593-2002
E-mail: Schifferbk@aol.com
Please visit our web site catalog at
www.SCHIFFERBOOKS.com

This book may be purchased from the publisher.
Include $3.95 for shipping. Please try your bookstore first.
We are always looking for people to write books on new and related subjects. If you have an idea for a book please contact us at the above address. You may write for a free catalog.

In Europe, Schiffer books are distributed by
Bushwood Books
6 Marksbury Avenue
Kew Gardens
Surrey TW9 4JF England
Phone: 44 (0) 20-8392-8585; Fax: 44 (0) 20-8392-9876
E-mail: Bushwd@aol.com
Free postage in the UK. Europe: air mail at cost.

Contents

Thank you, Donna Baker, for your wonderful organizational skills and for coming through with words when mine started to fail.

Updating your bath may be one of the easiest and most gratifying home improvement projects you can undertake. In a day you can switch towels, bath mats, and shower curtain to create a whole new look. You can elaborate by replacing a medicine cabinet with something new or antique to add character to the room. Or you might lay a new tile or resilient sheet floor – fairly easy projects that can be mastered by anyone. You might freshen the room with live plants or cut flowers, a new wastebasket, or a toothbrush holder. Or simply add new hand soaps and a pretty bottle of soap or skin conditioner.

Of course, the more elaborate projects come along every 20 years or so, when a bathroom's fixtures need replacing. That avocado green basin and lily orange tub may grow hard on the eyes. The glue behind the tile may be giving out, and the grouting looks downright gross. These needs necessitate an investment. And while you're at it, you might as well invest in the lifestyle of this oft-used room.

Consider whether back-massaging jets in a deep soaking tub wouldn't decrease your daily stress and improve your mental health. Or would a fresh shower stall save aggravation when it comes to cleaning time? Today's new homes often incorporate large bathing areas and antechamber areas with multiple sinks, not to mentioned overstuffed seating, custom cabinetry for the linens and toiletries, vanities for the daily beautifications, and even wardrobes where one dresses and undresses between work, play, and rest. Your local kitchen and bath designer may be able to incorporate a closet, or part of a guest room, to expand your bath area into a wonderful private retreat where your cares float away on a cloud of bubbles.

It never hurts to dream, in any case.

Asian Fusion

The Orient-inspired the geometric green panels that frame this wonderful bathroom antechamber and wardrobe area. A sleek stretch of custom cabinetry and composite countertop act in harmony with the modern design. *Courtesy of Brookhaven Cabinetry*

Modular bathroom furniture provides homeowners with a myriad of design possibilities. They are not permanent, but are moveable and interchangeable, allowing them to be used in numerous configurations over a lifetime. *Courtesy of Kohler Co.*

©*Everett & Soule*

Plain and simple Shinto inspiration give this expansive bathroom its exotic Asian atmosphere, dominated by a big Jacuzzi® whirlpool tub for two. *Courtesy of Jacuzzi Whirlpool Bath*

A shower and soaking/whirlpool tub invites one to engage in one of
Japan's most treasured traditions, cleansing both body and soul. This Zen-
inspired room keeps it simple, with an emphasis on meditative release.
Courtesy of Jacuzzi Whirlpool Bath

A curved Corian® alcove wall creates a dramatic backdrop for a pedestal sink and oval mirror. The sink is flanked by Yester-Tec maple vanities with space-saving drop-down leafs. *Photo courtesy of DuPont*

There's a strong Asian influence in the stacked cabinetry and wicker and raffia accents. *Courtesy of Decorá*

Natural wood tones, warm sky blue, and soft light work in harmony for this gentle, natural bathroom. *Courtesy of Brookhaven Cabinetry*

The outside was brought in for this amazing, two-story bathroom/solarium complete with a two-person Jacuzzi® whirlpool tub. Glass block separates more private areas of the bathroom while allowing the light in. *Courtesy of Jacuzzi Whirlpool Bath*

This bathroom works aesthetically, pairing natural wood tones in a pegged wall of boards and wonderful display cubbyholes. And when you open the cabinets, you find that they are saving space and energy as well, holding grooming tools near the mirror where they'll be used, and a stepping stool under the tallest cabinet for ease of access. *Courtesy of Merillat Industries*

The Old World feel of cast iron contrasts with sleek lines and basic forms. *Courtesy of Kohler Co.*

Chocolate walls allow a unique vanity unit to stand out as art. *Courtesy of Bis Bis Imports Boston*

Asian bamboo and a Japanese screen extend an invitation to soak away your cares on a broad expanse of wood decking. The hydrotherapy whirlpool tub includes thirty-two jets to create a rolling massage on the back while you ease your mind on a soft headrest. *Courtesy of Jacuzzi Whirlpool Bath*

Minimalism at its best, a simple basin tops a simple table, an exclamation point beneath a slash of mirror. *Courtesy of Duravit USA, Inc.*

A distinctively male influence dominates this washbasin and dressing table along with a matching, seven-drawer dresser. *Courtesy of Kohler Co.*

Simplicity of form and logical styling reduce the need for extras. A wall-mounted toilet and bidet, and a hand rinse basin occupy a minimum of space. Beyond, a sandblasted glass front opens at the slightest pull to reveal storage. *Courtesy of Duravit USA, Inc.*

Roman Baths

A tub offers a three-way vantage point through slider picture windows, crowned by an eyebrow slice of sky.
Courtesy of Simonton Windows

A neoclassical crown and column effect over the vanity give this bathroom palatial effect. Within the neutral finishes of cabinets, floor, and tile, glass-fronted cabinets allow easy color scheme change with the simple replacement of new towels. *Courtesy of Kraftmaid Cabinetry*

This bathroom
mimics the
classic Roman
bath, with fluted
columns and
domed ceiling. A
big picture
window and
hand-painted
topiary create a
garden environ-
ment, complete
with exposed
brick and plaster
on the "outside"
walls. A paneled
tub platform is lit
from below for
romantic effect.
*Courtesy of
Weather Shield
Windows &
Doors*

A columned row extends miles in the reflection of a vanity mirror. The Roman bath effect is underlined by pillared cabinetry and golden fixtures around the sink. *Courtesy of Decorá*

A polished black surround completes the circle created by an alcove, and a lion gives one the impression they've just entered an emperor's merry-go-round. A column-and-arches image in the leaded glass windows works to complete the Roman theme, adorned with gold accents and fixtures. *Courtesy of Jacuzzi Whirlpool Bath*

This neo-classical style is wildly popular in today's new Colonials, here complete with granite countertops, an arched alcove with decorative corbels, ornate molding over the countertop, and rich woodwork below. An elaborate, gilded sconce was mirror-mounted to double its glow. *Courtesy of StarMark Cabinetry*

Arches are repeated above window, mirror, and in a beautiful pedestal tub. Soft colors work with white for a soothing, relaxing environment. *Courtesy of Simonton Windows*

Bathe like a Roman emperor beneath neoclassical arch and columns, echoed in a modern acrylic-block window beyond. *Courtesy of Hy-Lite Products, Inc.*

Nearly a room in itself, this frameless glass shower enclosure has entrances on either side and a built-in bench for leisurely bathing. Stunning green tile includes mosaic work around the faucets and a wonderful arched top with recessed lighting. *Courtesy of Basco Shower Doors of Elegance*

A platform was built for a whirlpool tub, creating a pedestal on which a king or queen might linger, washing away a busy day's cares. Woodworking details are repeated in the tub pavilion, storage space below, and vanity on the far wall. *Courtesy of Wellborn Cabinet, Inc.*

The designer selected a black and white color scheme to make a dramatic statement with this bathroom. To maximize use of space, the tub surround is positioned right against the large glass shower enclosure. *Courtesy of Basco Shower Doors of Elegance*

A tile floor and art depicting Grecian urns contribute to this room's neoclassical atmosphere. *Courtesy of Congoleum Corp.*

A stately wardrobe/vanity room acts as entry chamber to a bathroom. *Courtesy of Wood-Mode Custom Cabinetry*

A bank of elegant cabinetry lines a hallway to the bath beyond. *Courtesy of Decorá*

Recessed squares on the walls of this birch lined, masterful bathroom are complemented by a tall, recessed window next to the shower. The wall treatment has been carried through to the expansive tub surround, which is topped by ceramic tile with plenty of room for the essential bath time accouterments. *Courtesy of Kohler Company, the Hardwood Council, and Kallista*

Marble makes this room rich, with tiles spanning floor, tub surround, and walls. The square of the tiles is echoed in the art on the wall, as well as an enormous, acrylic block window. *Courtesy of Hy-Lite Products, Inc.*

This tub feels like it enjoys a bigger space, magnified by a mirror and a bright wall of acrylic block. *Courtesy of Hy-Lite Products, Inc.*

This luxurious bathroom houses a medley of wonderful textures, from stucco walls to a velvet recliner and walnut-paneled whirlpool tub adorned with sleek gold fixtures. An oil painting above the tub creates a dramatic focal point. *Courtesy of Kohler Company and the Hardwood Council*

A sea of bright blue ceramic flooring greets the eye upon entering this spacious bathroom and contrasts wonderfully with the crisp white cabinetry. An abundance of glass-fronted cabinets provides lots of charm along with convenience. *Courtesy of Cabinets Plus*

Warm beige and ivory tones work throughout this room, creating consistency of design and an inviting atmosphere. *Courtesy of Congoleum Corp.*

Simple lines with lots of style work wonderfully here. Designer Brad Fortune placed tall graceful mirrors above hexagonal sinks and added an upholstered chair for textural interest. *Courtesy of Crystal Cabinet Works, Inc.*

A high window arches over custom cabinetry inset into this charming alcove. The result is natural light for a chamber reserved for the most intimate of company. *Courtesy of Brookhaven Cabinetry*

35

Neutral tones in the cabinetry, countertop, and wall paint allow this homeowner to re-accessorize on a whim. *Courtesy of Aristokraft*®

Generous molding and bead-board panels create a rich effect in this custom vanity, designed to ease the morning rush hour. *Courtesy of Wood-Mode Custom Cabinetry*

Custom-built cabinetry along one wall extends to encompass a big soaking tub. *Courtesy of Aristokraft®*

The tub is built into an elegant recess, adorned with arched ceiling and beaded glass window for light and privacy. Matching wood cabinetry completes the one-of-a-kind ambience. *Courtesy of Aristokraft®*

Blue finish on wood cabinetry makes a playful statement in this small but stately bathroom. *Courtesy of StarMark Cabinetry*

Two framed mirrors overlap above the vanity, stained to match custom cabinetry in this wonderful bathroom antechamber. *Courtesy of Decorá*

His and hers sinks are separated by a vanity area. Cabinetry creates an amazing storage area for towels, linens, and undergarments, surrounding a warm room where two can work together getting ready for the world, or bidding it good night. *Courtesy of Schrock Cabinets*

A central storage area creates vanity areas for him and her in this spacious
bathroom. *Courtesy of Diamond Cabinets*

Peach and rhubarb tones form a yummy background to frost-stained cabinetry and creamy white fixtures. *Courtesy of Schrock Cabinets*

Country Style

A bright corner unit creates his and hers sinks, set against a country blue backdrop.
Courtesy of Decorá

Rustic flair in the wood moldings and the homespun textiles are perfect for this weekend home. *Courtesy of Decorá*

An update on the old pie-safe, this custom bathroom hutch is a wonderful way to store and display bathroom linens. *Courtesy of Wood-Mode Custom Cabinetry*

Blue and white never become outdated with home decorators. *Courtesy of Congoleum Corp.*

Charming effect is created with reclaimed lumber and nautical antiques. The fixtures capture the look and feel of designs dating back to an earlier era while providing modern comforts and efficiencies. *Courtesy of Kohler Co.*

Cozy without being confining, this bathroom under the eaves combines warm oak flooring with delicate floral wallpaper and matching window treatment. Natural light pours in through the wide window above the tub. *Courtesy of Kohler Company and the Hardwood Council*

Shaker style cabinetry and the grooved wallboard have a light, taupe glaze that give this bathroom its bright, country atmosphere. The neutral colors allow for quick make-overs – the open cubicles show off towels or display items. *Courtesy of Kraftmaid Cabinetry*

A bevy of frosted glass squares lets soft light permeate this generously proportioned bathroom. *Courtesy of Portland Cement Association*

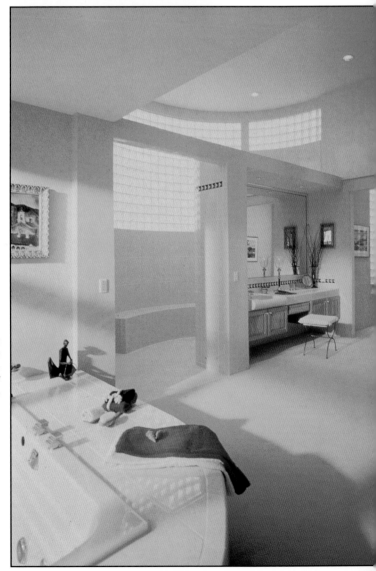

A blue finish on wood and two-tone paint on the wall evokes a simple, old-world place. *Courtesy of Bis Bis Imports Boston*

A window seat offers an invitation to relax and enjoy the morning sun. *Courtesy of Yorktowne Cabinets*

A shared dressing area can be a place to relax, have a private chat, or to rush through the morning routine side-by-side. *Courtesy of Yorktowne Cabinets*

Courtesy of Yorktowne Cabinets

Arts and Crafts style cabinetry is crowned by decorative display cases. *Courtesy of Decora*

A look typifying the best of the old West – unmilled log beams, rough-painted brick, a Navajo rug, and of course the boots – is lent an air of refinement by handsome cherry cabinetry. *Courtesy of MasterBrand Cabinets®*

Contemporary

A custom-designed sink and bath surround
add contemporary flair to this bath setting.
Photo courtesy of DuPont

When a luxurious master bath becomes an overwhelming desire, a converted spare bedroom fills the bill. Tiger maple wood, glass block shower walls, and creamy Corian® solid surfaces blend together to produce a tranquil oasis. *Photo courtesy of DuPont*

Frameless cabinetry curves around a sink in an offset corner unit. *Courtesy of Bis Bis Imports Boston*

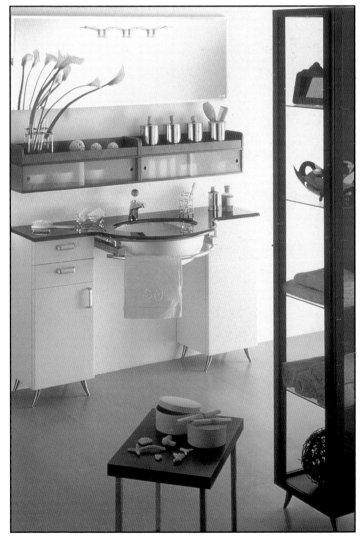

A glass console around the sink and frosted glass in the cabinet faces above contribute to the 21st Century feel of this sleek lavatory station. *Courtesy of Bis Bis Imports Boston*

Marble and glass create an impressive, palatial master bath. A Jacuzzi® whirlpool tub was placed on a raised platform to take advantage of an amazing view. *Courtesy of Jacuzzi Whirlpool Bath*

Color is confined almost exclusively to the green glass console around the sink and the frosted blue doors on a free standing cabinet and wall shelf. *Courtesy of Bis Bis Imports Boston*

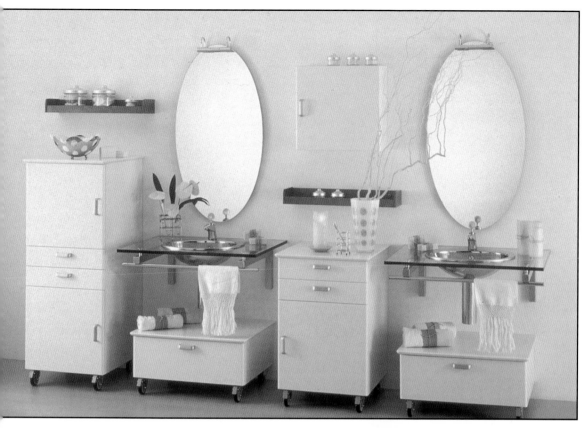

Twin work stations carve out marital territory and create an echoing statement in style. *Courtesy of Bis Bis Imports Boston*

Light takes center stage here, with a large wall of frosted glass reflected in the expansive mirror. The linear motif of the square panes is softened by a scalloped design incorporated into oak cabinets below the dual sinks. *Courtesy of the Hardwood Council*

Playful curves are plentiful – around a whimsical mirror, down the side of the vanity, and where the cabinet doors come together – in this combination bathroom/dressing area. *Photo courtesy of DuPont*

A silver shower stall frames a corner display of three-inch, Cross-Colors® mosaic tiles – noticeably smaller than the usual four-inch tiles, and much easier to maintain than tiny, one-inch mosaic tiles. *Courtesy of Crossville Porcelain Stone/USA*

Warm and cool colors were selected to create a clean contrast with white fixtures in this New York City bathroom renovation. Recessed, mirrored cabinets above the maple vanity visually enlarge the space and create two handy niches below to facilitate open storage of bath essentials. Green mosaic glass tiles covering the walls and floor incorporate the colors of nature and blend effortlessly with the chrome fixtures and accessories. *Courtesy of Victoria Benatar Urban*

Photography by David Taylor/Stylist: Raul Flores/Project Designer: Victoria Benatar Urban

Top left and bottom left: Two variations on a theme, chunky white fixtures reflect in glossy blue tile, with a dividing wall for privacy. *Courtesy of Duravit USA, Inc.*

Free-standing storage unites are in keeping with the simplistic design of this modern bathroom. *Courtesy of Duravit USA, Inc.*

Smooth travertine slabs were used to cover all surfaces in this bathroom, interrupted only by a band of rectangular mirrors encircling the room. Dying the vanity and mirror above the same bold blue as the adjoining bedroom achieves dramatic effect while creating continuity between the spaces. The vanity's counter was extended with a small travertine shelf over the bathtub to integrate the two as one long surface. *Project Designer: Victoria Benatar Urban*

A corner tub stands flanked by glass walls, ready to offer soothing whirlpool relief for two. *Courtesy of Jacuzzi Whirlpool Bath*

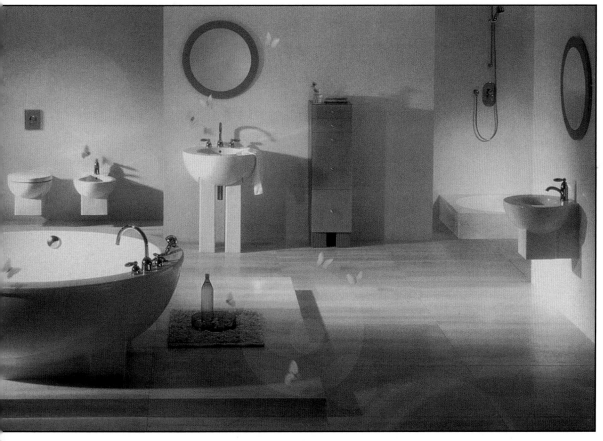

Princeton architect Michael Graves calls this his Dreamscape, a postmodern bathroom with echoing shapes in a pastel pallet. *Courtesy of Duravit USA, Inc.*

In all that he designs, Philippe Starck strives for the ingeniously simple. Here stucco forms a backdrop for elegant fixtures atop a painted wood floor. *Courtesy of Duravit USA, Inc.*

Cameron M. Snyder, C

John A. Buscarello, AS

Wall-mounted cabinets appear to float above the floor, adding an airy quality to this bright little bathroom. A right-hand medicine cabinet is concealed behind a pane of frosted glass. *Photo courtesy of DuPont*

Opposite page: An amazing bathroom, this one has it all – steam room, sauna, whirlpool tub, and a glass-top vanity that is an artwork in itself. *Courtesy of Wood-Mode Custom Cabinetry*

Masculine

A look-through fireplace illuminates both bedroom and bath. A striking red tub is sunken in a concrete surround, which works with concrete tiles in floor and shower. *Courtesy of Get Real Surfaces*

Sleek modern bathroom furnishings feature frosted glass fronts that pop
open easily to reveal storage space. *Courtesy of Duravit USA, Inc.*

Man-high cabinets become architectural elements in this bath where
minimalism is the rule. *Courtesy of Bis Bis Imports Boston*

Separating sinks from shower and toilet areas allows for increased traffic in the bathroom, and quickens the morning routine for couples and families. *Courtesy of Hy-Lite Products, Inc.*

Questech® Metals real metal tile and a sidewall of mirror add space to a room limited in size. *Courtesy of Crossville Porcelain Stone/USA*

Photo by James F. Wilson

Rich shades of brown and beige are blended and juxtaposed for a bathroom with a masculine feel. *Courtesy of Crossville Porcelain Stone/USA*

A steely blue floor underlines a creative approach in this powder room, where metallic stars, a sand dollar, and suspended ribbons adorn a rough-finish wall over white wainscoting. *Courtesy of Crossville Porcelain Stone/USA*

A glass-walled shower maintains a surreal presence in a lengthy master bath, underlined by earth-toned tile. *Courtesy of Crossville Porcelain Stone/USA*

Neighbors weren't a concern when this homeowner built a spot for soaking that encompassed a sweeping mountain view. Rather, it was privacy within the home that motivated the acrylic blocks around the shower stall and on diagonal windows that might afford a peek from people on the nearby patio. *Courtesy of Hy-Lite Products, Inc.*

This playful bathroom motif adds a royal twist, with dramatic red border over black and white stripes, and royal blue linens and accents. *Courtesy of Style Solutions* ™

A prominently positioned whirlpool leaves no doubt that this bathroom is a haven of relaxation. *Courtesy of Portland Cement Association*

A fascinating photo print on tile creates a streambed appearance for the floor. Another interesting effect is found in the African Wenge wood cabinetry, which works with changing sunlight throughout the day to create anything from a plum cast to a blue, cocoa, or silvery gray. *Courtesy of Interni/ABODE*

Feminine Florals

A decorative wall is multifunctional – it serves as a privacy barrier for the bather and a wonderful open storage unit for linens on one side, a closet on the other. *Courtesy of Congoleum Corp.*

An intimate, private corner was created using rich dark tones in textiles and rich cherry wood. *Courtesy of Decorá*

The sink and vanity were brought into the
bedroom here to save space in the bathroom.
This also allows two people to get ready in the
morning. *Courtesy of Decorá*

A feminine touch in color and detail makes this Her Hideaway, complete with claw-foot tub for a romantic soak by the colorful light of leaded glass windows. A seven-foot wardrobe on the right is the perfect place for her most intimate wear. *Courtesy of Aristokraft®*

Sentimental favorites are showcased in this vanity area, from a child's high chair, to an old family portrait, and a collection of porcelain mementoes. Custom cabinetry conceals the more mundane items of day-to-day hygiene. *Courtesy of Brookhaven Cabinetry*

Lit recesses over custom cabinetry mirror the arched window over the vanity area. This bathroom antechamber is packed with storage space for linens, toiletries, and lingerie. *Courtesy of Brookhaven Cabinetry*

An elegant bathroom is defined by curved custom cabinetry, an arched window, and a sweeping wallpaper design that graces the high ceilings. *Courtesy of StarMark Cabinetry*

A wonderful stretch of custom cabinetry provides luxurious storage. A display area on the right breaks the line and adds interest. *Courtesy of StarMark Cabinetry*

An antique finish adds an aura of continuity to this spacious vanity area. Reflected beyond is a bold swag over the windows floating above a bathing area with a view. *Courtesy of Field-stone Cabinetry*

A wonderful, emerald green floor inspired a room rich in mint and peach tones. The white structural elements – fixtures, slatted linen closet doors, and window treatments stand out in feminine contrast. *Courtesy of Congoleum Corp.*

A window-side soak is framed by rich linens, underlined by a harlequin pattern in resilient sheet flooring. *Courtesy of Congoleum Corp.*

It's all in the view, or rather, it's underneath, where cabinetry creates an underline for bright windows opening to a private yard. Room on the wall was reserved, of course, for a view of the occupant. *Courtesy of Diamond Cabinets*

Perennial favorites wherever tile and paint can be found, blue and white are united for cheerful contrast. *Courtesy of Brookhaven Cabinetry*

A drop ceiling lighting unit defines a vanity area within a room of tall walls and big windows. *Courtesy of Brookhaven Cabinetry*

An expansive washroom provides marital bliss, with separate walls for his and hers activities, joined at the center by storage space. *Courtesy of Fieldstone Cabinetry*

A corner tub invites the weary to linger and soak in a great view. Matching cabinetry creates a tub surround as well as adjacent storage space. *Courtesy of StarMark Cabinetry*

Although the floral theme is consistent throughout this room, it isn't powerful enough to drive a manly man away. The buds have been carefully contained among conservative colors, underlined by masculine, faux marble tile in resilient sheet flooring. *Courtesy of Congoleum Corp.*

Luxurious storage space allows all those little essentials, as well as big towels and bottles, to be packed neatly out of sight. *Courtesy of Yorktowne Cabinets*

The serviceable wall tambour cabinet and lighted tri-view medicine cabinet are prominently capped with decorative crown molding for a fine furniture effect. *Courtesy of Yorktowne Cabinets*

Step up to comfort and elegance in this V-shaped bathroom decorated in warm shades of cream, beige, and cocoa. A sink with a pretty floral skirt is positioned below the steps, leaving the main portion of the bathroom uncluttered and open. Textured carpeting leading to the bedroom contrasts nicely with the sleek maple flooring. *Courtesy of Kohler Company and the Hardwood Council*

A monochromatic color scheme and tall windows overlooking the garden lend a soothing touch to this simply appointed but very stylish bathroom. *Courtesy of the Hardwood Manufacturers Association and the Hardwood Council*

A corner cabinet on the tub surround creates a nook for storing towels and bath supplies. Urethane millwork around the tub, windows, and shower door add attractive detailing to the room. *Courtesy of Style Solutions, Inc.*

Hand-painted roses climb the walls and wend their way amidst arched windows. Beneath this bright display, a Jacuzzi® snuggles in a frame of custom-built cabinetry. *Courtesy of Jacuzzi Whirlpool Bath*

A whirlpool retreat perches by picture windows, opening a wood-land view to a soaking occupant. *Courtesy of Jacuzzi Whirlpool Bath*

Bead-board wainscoting and wood flooring define this room's age-old design. Above the chair rail, recessed shelf space has been created to work naturally within the decor. *Courtesy of Kohler Co.*

Two wash stations lead toward the bathroom's inner sanctum, creating his and her areas within easy earshot. *Courtesy of Diamond Cabinets*

Romantic

A woman's vanity was custom built with classic styling and antique finish, surrounded by rich color and texture for her boudoir retreat. *Courtesy of Decorá*

A huge swath of mirror over light cabinetry creates contrast against an exotic pallet of dark tones. *Courtesy of Brookhaven Cabinetry*

An arch is such a beautiful thing, set amidst the straight lines and square rooms of the average home. Here the effect of an arched window was maximized with a built-in overhang complete with hanging lamp. *Courtesy of Weather Shield Windows & Doors*

Fresh flowers make cheerful friends, here dancing around a window-lit tub in bud vases. *Courtesy of Weather Shield Windows & Doors*

This room was designed for water lovers, offering the opportunity to enjoy both a romantic fire as well as television and music while soaking in a whirlpool tub. Two ergonomic loungers each offer three stacked back jets and, at the other end, an extra large foot jet for head-to-toe hydrotherapy. *Courtesy of Jacuzzi Whirlpool Bath*

Tucked under an eaves, this bath gains elegance from classic elements including cherry cabinetry, Grecian urns, and a floral border paper over marbled walls. *Courtesy of Yorktowne Cabinets*

Crafted to imitate freestanding furniture, this custom cabinet unit creates work stations for hygiene and beauty routines. *Courtesy of Yorktowne Cabinets*

This sumptuous bathroom with Roman style pillars and a raised tub was designed by Stan Ward. Wonderful mosaic tile work has been incorporated into the wall treatment and the tub surround. *Courtesy of Crystal Cabinet Works, Inc.*

97

Spot Color

This practical bath separates the sink and makeup areas and incorporates plenty of built-in storage in a minimum amount of space. *Courtesy of Yorktowne Cabinets*

Earthen tile tones and blu
blinds give this room a
natural cast. Natural wood
cabinetry conceals an
enviable stretch of storag
space. *Courtesy of
StarMark Cabinetry*

Cubbyholes in custom cabinetry
allow for a playful display of towels.
An ottoman creates moveable
seating options, whether by the
vanity, or next to the tub when
someone special needs a scrub.
Courtesy of Congoleum Corp.

This room starts with solid basics in wallpaper and resilient sheet flooring, and adds accents in burgundy and gold. *Courtesy of Congoleum Corp.*

102   An eggplant glass console around the sink lines up with a stripe of shag carpeting and a set of
bath towels to celebrate with sunset pink on the walls. *Courtesy of Bis Bis Imports Boston*

Clean ivory and bright golden hues make this a wonderful place to wake up to. A corner whirlpool tub makes it a great place to wind down at the end of the day, too. *Courtesy of Yorktowne Cabinets*

Mixed elements add up to feminine charm in this room, from the claw-footed tub to the fancy cutouts in the bridge over custom-made cabinetry. *Courtesy of Yorktowne Cabinets*

Decorative fabric was sewn onto towels and an ottoman, working with colors in the walls and cabinetry along with the flooring and countertops to tie this room together. A divider wall has been put to use as vanity and storage unit, while helping to divide the room into work zones for the morning rush. *Courtesy of Congoleum Corp.*

Yellow accents work with gray in wallpaper and the resilient flooring, which evokes a mosaic tile effect while remaining warm to the bare foot. *Courtesy of Congoleum Corp.*

Neutral tones in wall, floor, and fixtures allow the homeowner to accessorize according to whim or season. *Courtesy of Congoleum Corp.*

Opposite page: Russet accents contrast with a natural finish on the maple cabinetry. Peek-a-boo cubbyholes and pull drawers allow the homeowner to play with the color theme while keeping washcloths handy. *Courtesy of Decorá*

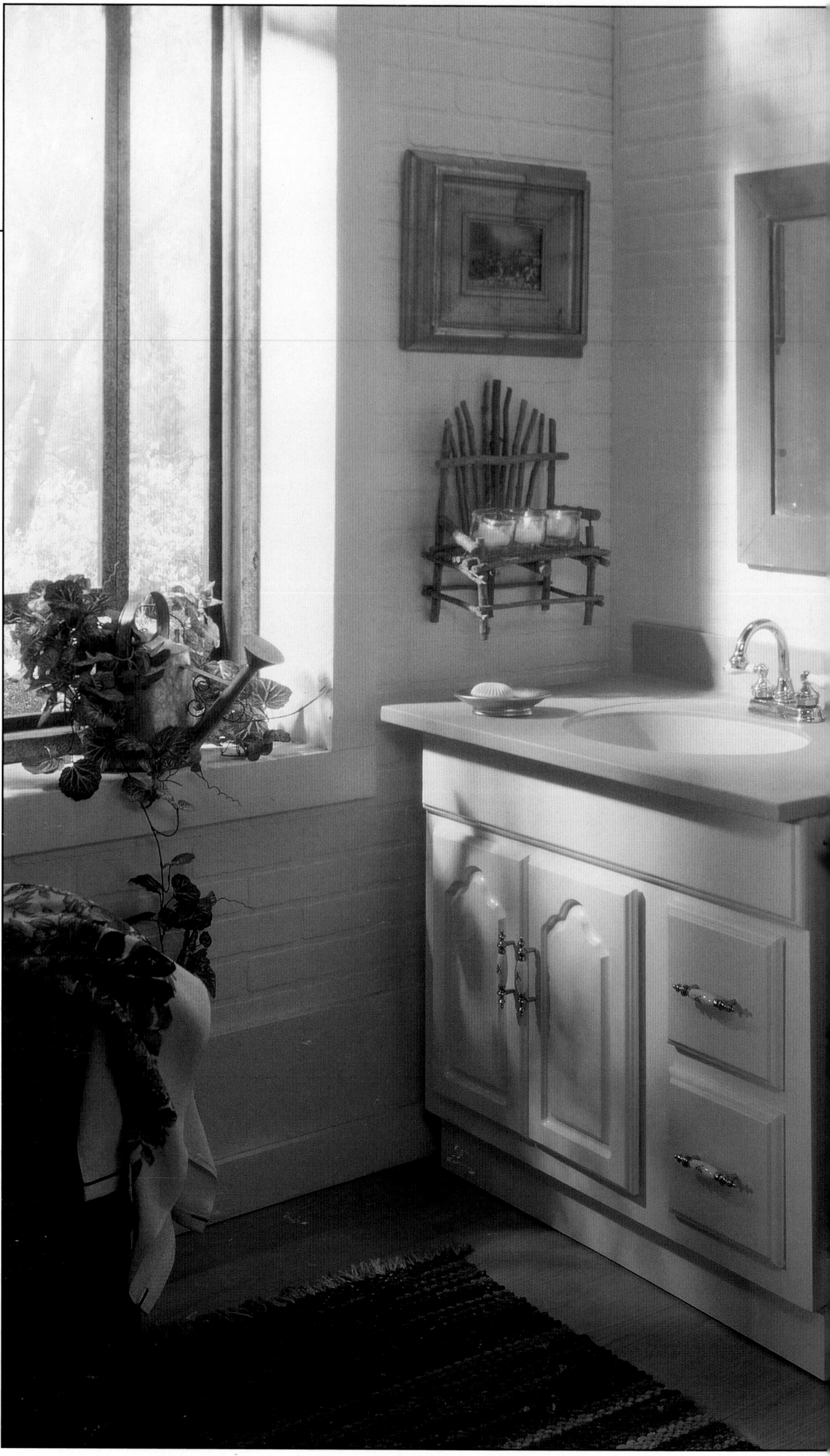

A collection of antique mirrors adds charm to a bathroom corner. A traditional vanity and reproduction chest provide ample storage for toiletries. *Photo courtesy of DuPont*

Designer Philippe Starck invites you to linger in the bathroom, creating a simple retreat in this reclaimed warehouse where you can bathe by a warm fire, or give yourself a pedicure while rocked back in a wooden chair. *Courtesy of Duravit USA, Inc.*

Opposite page: Painted to evoke the feeling of a billowy tent, this camper roughs it under a crystal chandelier. A tub-filled alcove is a luxurious retreat, complete with whirlpool jets to soothe tired muscles. *Courtesy of Jacuzzi Whirlpool Bath*

Tiles below match the brick arches in the vaulted ceiling. A space set aside for the rituals of daily hygiene was left pure in its simplicity by designer Philippe Starck. *Courtesy of Duravit USA, Inc.*

n enormous painting, an original stucco wall, and a scattered tile attern mark this territory unique.
Courtesy of Duravit USA, Inc.

A rich atmosphere was created here, using generous wood-trimmed windows, brick-like tiles for the wainscoting, and wallpaper with a coppery gleam.
Courtesy of Weather Shield Windows & Doors

Stylish and refined in nature, this lovely bathroom is highlighted by three large mirrors, double sinks separated by a generously proportioned vanity area, and storage space galore. *Courtesy of Cabinets Plus*

Tucked into a cozy atrium, this combination exterior shower with jacuzzi pool works perfectly for private relaxation or casual entertaining. Using the existing levels on the site, the shower was created flush with the floors to keep the whirlpool mechanism located under the wooden deck. When not needed for actual bathing, the shower can be used to provide the soothing, peaceful sound of cascading water. *Project Designer: Victoria Benatar Urban*

A stylized wave design on the glass shower enclosure adds a bit of whimsy to this artfully designed bathroom. Frosted glass squares on one-half of the shower provide wonderful design contrast, while an emphasis on glass rather than metal keeps the bathroom visually open and spacious. *Courtesy of Basco Shower Doors of Elegance*

Playful details – a checked floor, a striped tub surround and wainscoting add color to this elegant bathroom. *Courtesy of Yorktowne Cabinets*

Bold use of texture characterizes this softly lit bathroom. The designer played stuccoed walls and rough-hewn wood in the corner against a silky smooth maple vanity with gleaming gold fixtures. *Courtesy of Crystal Cabinet Works, Inc.*

His and her sinks share a vanity in a spacious bathroom antechamber, complete with lots of pull drawers for linens and bath accessories. *Courtesy of Wood-Mode Custom Cabinetry*

Opposite page: An artful assembly of squares – black, white, and wood – creates a corner of conspicuous interest. The vanity itself was crafted to look like an old drop-leaf table, with a washbasin on top, only this basin has a drain. *Courtesy of Wood-Mode Custom Cabinetry*

Peggy McGowan, CKD, CBD, ASID/Stanley Hura

Miscellaneous Master Baths

A decorator used bold strokes in this richly toned room, where snow-white fixtures stand in pleasing contrast with burnt umber walls and forest green draperies. *Courtesy of Kohler Co.*

Antique cabinetry, wide-plank flooring, and painted wainscoting add charm to this straightforward little bathroom, brightened by yellow tones in paint and fixtures. *Courtesy of Kohler Co.*

Warm tones on the walls work with a cream finish on the pedestal lavatory and toilet to create a soothing atmosphere. This small bath embraces simplicity, allowing the simple lines of the fixtures, and a single blossom, to achieve an identity. *Courtesy of Kohler Co.*

Clean, white, and wonderful. Besides these three recommendations, there's another reason why you'll want to linger in this bathroom. In the corner stands a combination whirlpool bath, shower system and steam bath built for two. Besides two body jets and two lumbar jets, two multifunction showerheads, and eight vertical body sprays, there is a built-in stereo/CD system complete with four speakers and a television. *Courtesy of Jacuzzi Whirlpool Bath*

Neat squares of acrylic block allow light into a small bathroom and create an illusion of height. A longer window on the left helps ease the claustrophobia of sitting in a small tub in a small corner. *Courtesy of Hy-Lite Products, Inc.*

A master bath with an artful touch, this room gains visual space from the mirrored wall on one side and a glass shower stall in the corner. The designer also incorporated a large, separate dressing area. *Courtesy of Portland Cement Association*

Cross-Colors® mosaics, shiny gold hardware, and flesh-tone fixtures mix for exotic, retro effect. *Courtesy of Crossville Porcelain Stone/USA*

This bathroom defines quaint and cozy. A footed tub enjoys an idyllic view of the countryside by day, and the enchanting lights of a chandelier by night. *Courtesy of Weather Shield Windows & Doors*

Questech® Metals tiles define an exotic pampering place in a luxuriously appointed bath. A place designed for leisurely pedicures and hot oil treatments. *Courtesy of Crossville Porcelain Stone/USA*

A corner design allows smaller bathrooms to accommodate a whirlpool bath big enough for two. *Courtesy of Jacuzzi Whirlpool Bath*

127

Wall-to-wall, this vanity unit creates a great stretch of counter space. There's plenty of room for both faces in this mirror. *Courtesy of Wood-Mode Custom Cabinetry*

Scalloping around the sink is echoed in the mirror frame. *Courtesy of Duravit USA, Inc.*

Mirrors on three sides of two sinks allow a couple to complete their morning ablutions without competition for space or view. *Courtesy of Decorá*

Frameless custom cabinetry with white laminate finish creates a sleek, modern feel in this appealing vanity area. *Courtesy of Brookhaven Cabinetry*

Cool and clean, this tub was set diagonally in a corner made bright by acrylic blocks, which make it possible to grow plants in the bathroom without inviting peepers to the panes. *Courtesy of Hy-Lite Products, Inc.*

Here's a wonderful retreat – a big, step up platform to a sunken tub spacious enough for a long soak. A three-sided wall of windows allows in light while insuring privacy. *Courtesy of Hy-Lite Products, Inc.*

Wonderful colors work together in the granite tub surround, the ivory tub and acrylic block windows. *Courtesy of Hy-Lite Products, Inc.*

Tile and block act together for a geometric effect. This built-in shower includes a seating area and floor-level entry to accommodate special needs. *Courtesy of Hy-Lite Products, Inc.*

Carpet was continued up the sides of this built-in tub and step to soften and warm a soaring space. *Courtesy of Hy-Lite Products, Inc.*

Who wouldn't dream of such a bathroom, with a pedestal tub set high on a platform, lots of storage, and streaming light that works its way from sun through two walls of acrylic block to illuminate a private toilet and shower area. *Courtesy of Hy-Lite Products, Inc.*

Lit acrylic blocks surround twin mirrors over pedestal sinks. A built-in vanity shelf behind the sinks is both functional and decorative. *Courtesy of Hy-Lite Products, Inc.*

Photography by David Schilling

To create a bathroom with the look of furniture, designer Jim Bishop Jr. used maple vanities with furniture style feet, custom mouldings, and ornamental inlays. A spice finish with chocolate glaze adds warmth to the cabinetry. *Courtesy of Jim Bishop Cabinets, Inc.*

Opposite page: A narrow shower stall gets added glamour with floor-to-ceiling tiles and a privacy window that lets the sun shine in without giving the neighbors a glimpse. *Courtesy of Hy-Lite Products, Inc.*

A once ordinary bathroom becomes exciting with quadruple tile borders at the ceiling depicting creatures from the sea. The theme is carried through to the tile work around the sink. *Courtesy of M.E. Tile Company, Inc.*

Coordinating tile work on all surfaces of this bathroom adds wonderful pizzazz. A simple gray and white color scheme is easy on the eyes and doesn't overwhelm the terrific designs. *Courtesy of M.E. Tile Company, Inc.*

An eye-catching mural with seashell design is the focal point of this tiled wall done in warm shades of orange. The mural's border design is repeated at the juncture of the wall and ceiling. *Courtesy of M.E. Tile Company, Inc.*

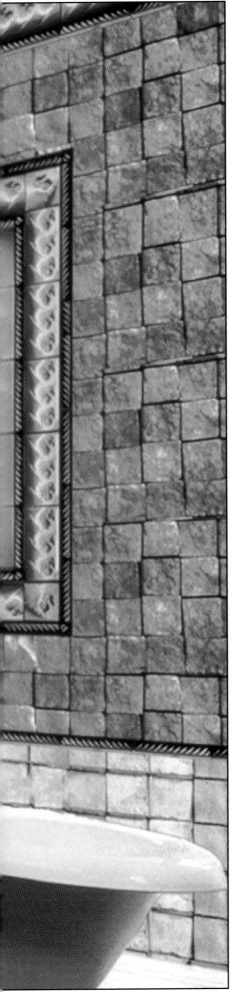

Seating options include a deep soak in a tub or a padded bench by the window. In between, a spacious shower stall offers wall-mounted and hand-held options for head-to-toe cleansing. *Courtesy of Basco Shower Doors of Elegance*

Decorative moldings jazz up a room. If you've got over eight feet of wall, don't be afraid to install five or more inches of built-up crown molding. *Courtesy of Style Solutions, Inc.*

137

Aristokraft®
One Master Brand Cabinets Dr.
Jasper, IN 47546
812-482-2527
www.aristokraft.com
Aristokraft is a leading manufacturer of quality kitchen, bath, and home cabinetry. From the traditional beauty of oak to the radiant elegance of cherry, the company offers more than forty different styles and a multitude of accessories.

Basco Shower Doors of Elegance
7201 Snider Road
Mason, OH 45040
513-573-1900
In business since 1955, Basco Shower Doors of Elegance manufactures standard and custom designed shower and tub enclosures. The company offers a wide selection of innovative glass, frame, and color options to complement today's diverse bath decors.

Bis Bis Imports Boston
4 Park Plaza
Boston, MA 02116
617-350-7565
www.bisbis.com
Bis Bis bath furnishings are handcrafted from solid walnut and feature marble pulls, hand-blown Murano glass sconces, glass console sinks, and a full range of modular furnishings and accessories.

Brookhaven Cabinetry
One Second Street
Kreamer, PA 17833
800-635-7500
www.wood-mode.com
A companion line of Wood-Mode, Brookhaven provides semi-custom cabinetry in styles ranging from country to contemporary and traditional to high-tech. Their finishes provide an ideal blend of toughness and beauty.

Cabinets Plus
1086 Route 58
Riverhead, NY 11901
631-727-8062
Lou Nardolillo has served the Hamptons area of New York for the last fourteen years and feels his commitment to customer satisfaction has been fundamental to his success. Lou is a Certified Kitchen Designer, accredited through the National Kitchen and Bath Association.

Congoleum Corp.
Department C
P.O. Box 3127
Mercerville, NJ 08619-0127
800-274-3266
www.congoleum.com
One of the nation's leading manufacturers of resilient sheet and tile, resilient wood plank, and laminate flooring for more than one hundred years. All products are designed and manufactured in New Jersey, Pennsylvania, and Maryland.

Crossville Porcelain Stone/USA
PO Box 1168
Crossville, TN 38557
931-484-2110
www.crossville-ceramics.com
Founded in 1986, this is the largest domestic manufacturer of porcelain stone tile for both residential and contract applications, and the exclusive distributor of Questech® Metals tiles and borders.

Crystal Cabinet Works, Inc.
1100 Crystal Drive
Princeton, MN 55371-3368
800-347-5045
763-389-5846
www.ccworks.com
Founded in 1947, Crystal Cabinet Works, Inc. is considered one of the top independent custom cabinet manufacturers in the United States. Crystal offers two custom lines of cabinetry: Crystal®, and Quest®, and a commercial line of custom cabinetry.

Diamond Cabinets
One Master Brand Cabinets Dr.
Jasper, IN 47546
812-482-2527
www.aristokraft.com
Style, quality, and choices ... Diamond provides quality cabinetry, offering current styles and popular storage and organization accessories for consumers who want to balance functionality, beauty, and price.

Distinctive Kitchen & Bath Interiors
5891 Firestone Drive
Syracuse, NY 13206
315-434-9011/Fax: 434-9013
www.idistinctiveinteriors.com
bfagan@idistinctiveinteriors.com (Brian K. Fagan)
Design consultant Brian K. Fagan has been creating kitchen and bath designs for central New York clients since 1990. His designs have been featured in *Better Homes & Gardens* and in *Kitchens by Professional Designers*.

DuPont Corian®
P.O. Box 80012
Barley Mill Plaza — Building 12
Wilmington, DE 19880-0012
1-800-426-7426
www.corian.com
DuPont's Corian® surfaces offer timeless beauty and performance to suit a variety of design needs. Solid surfaces by Corian® help create warm, inviting rooms.

DuPont Zodiaq®
P.O. Box 80012
Barley Mill Plaza — Building 12
Wilmington, Delaware 19880-0016
1-877-229-3935
www.zodiaq.com
DuPont's Zodiaq® surfaces offer timeless beauty and performance to suit a variety of design needs. Zodiaq® quartz surfaces are just right for an elegant, contemporary look.

Duravit USA, Inc.
1750 Breckinridge Parkway, Suite 500
Duluth, Georgia 30096
770-931-3575
www.duravit.com
Dating back to a German earthenware factory established in 1817, Duravit has focused on production of high-quality bathroom furniture and accessories. Designers of international renown and authorities in the field of bathroom aesthetics work for the company.

Fieldstone, Inc.
600 E. 48th St. N.
Sioux Falls, SD 57104
605-335-8600
www.StarMarkCabinetry.com
Fine Fieldstone cabinetry offers choices to let you express yourself with full creative freedom. Choose from a comprehensive selection of woods, finishes, accessories, fashion elements, and true custom options.

Get Real Surfaces
37 West 20th Street Suite 304
New York, NY 10011
212-414-1620
Get Real Surfaces will create virtually anything that can be designed
and made out of concrete, in any color. Product lines include kitchen
countertops and vanities with integral sinks, floor material and tubs,
tiles, fireplaces, and architectural details.

The Hardwood Council
P.O. Box 525
Oakmont, PA 15139
412-281-4980
www.hardwoodcouncil.com
The Hardwood Council produces free technical literature on working
with North American hardwoods. Interior designers, architects, build-
ers, and remodelers are invited to view and order the Council's literature on their website.

Hy-Lite Products, Inc.
101 California Avenue
Beaumont, CA 92223
1-800-827-3691
www.hy-lite.com
Acrylic block windows are about 70 percent lighter than glass, and Hy-
Lite can custom make windows in almost any size and shape, and
guarantee against cracking, flaking, chipping, or discoloration.

Interni/ABODE
50 Terminal Street
Charlestown, MA 02129
617-242-4140
www.interniusa.com
This collaborative of architects and designers works closely with clients
to successfully realize every project regardless of size. They consider
monetary constraints, respect the need for value, and believe in the
possibility to design without compromise.

Jacuzzi Whirlpool Bath
2121 N. California Boulevard
Walnut Creek, CA 94596
925-938-7070
www.jacuzzi.com
Jacuzzi has been turning heads ever since it created the world's first
whirlpool bath. The company continues to make innovative strides in
hydrotherapy with luxurious whirlpool baths, shower systems, and
bathroom suites.

Jim Bishop Cabinets, Inc.
P.O. Box 11424
Montgomery, AL 36111
800-410-2444, ext. 3017
www.jimbishopcabinets.com
Jim Bishop founded the company in 1964. Door styles are available in oak, maple, poplar, cherry, thermofoil, and melamine. Six standard finishes are offered as well as glazes, semi-opaque base coats, crackle, edge wear, and veiling.

Kohler Co.
Kohler, WI 53044
800-4-Kohler
www.kohler.com
Founded in 1873, it is one of the oldest and largest privately held companies in the United States. It markets its products under the brand names of Kohler, Sterling, Kallista, Ann Sacks, Robern, Canac and, in Europe, under Jacob Delafon, Neomediam, and Sanijura.

Kraftmaid Cabinetry, Inc.
15535 South State Avenue
Middlefield, Ohio 44062
440-632-2389
www.kraftmaid.com
The nation's largest built-to-order/semi-custom cabinetry manufacturer, KraftMaid's extensive product lines include more than 90 door styles in a variety of hardwoods and laminates.

M.E. Tile Company, Inc.
6463 Waveland Ave.
Hammond, IN 46320
219-554-1877
www.metile.com
M. E. Tile Company, Inc. produces hand made, sculptured, low relief, ceramic tile suitable for kitchens, bathrooms, foyers, fireplaces, door and window frames. Over 500 raised relief single tile moldings, liners, mural, linear arrays, and arches are available in many different glaze surfaces and colors.

Merillat Industries
5353 West U.S. Highway 223
Adrian, MI 49221
517-263-0771
www.merrillat.com
The largest manufacturer of cabinetry for the entire home in North America since 1985, with eleven manufacturing plants in the United States. Product lines include Organomics™, Amera, Merillat, and Woodward.